HOW DID THEY BUILD THAT? HOW DID THEY BUILD THAT? HOW DID THEY BUILD THAT? HOW DID THEY BUILD THAT?

HOW DID THEY BUILD THAT?

STADIUM

BY MATT MULLINS

COMMUNITY · CONNECTIONS

Published in the United States of America by Cherry Lake Publishing
Ann Arbor, Michigan
www.cherrylakepublishing.com

Content Adviser: Nancy Kristof
Reading Adviser: Cecilia Minden-Cupp, PhD, Literacy Consultant

Photo Credits: Cover and page 1, ©Lauren Cameo, used under license from Shutterstock, Inc.; page 5, ©Marcelo Saavedra, used under license from Shutterstock, Inc.; page 7, ©Rob Wilson, used under license from Shutterstock, Inc.; page 9, ©Clynt Garnham/Alamy; page 11, ©yuyangc, used under license from Shutterstock, Inc.; page 13, ©Jason Stitt, used under license from Shutterstock, Inc.; page 15, ©djapeman, used under license from Shutterstock, Inc.; page 17, ©London Aerial Photo Library/Alamy; page 19, ©Susan Law Cain, used under license from Shutterstock, Inc.; page 21, ©David Lee, used under license from Shutterstock, Inc.

LIBRARY OF CONGRESS CATALOGING-IN-PUBLICATION DATA
Mullins, Matt.
How did they build that? Stadium / by Matt Mullins.
p. cm.—(Community connections)
Includes index.
ISBN-13: 978-1-60279-489-4
ISBN-10: 1-60279-489-8
Stadiums—Design and construction—Juvenile literature. I. Title.
II. Title: Stadium. III. Series.
TH4714.M85 2009
690'.5827—dc22 2008049361

Cherry Lake Publishing would like to acknowledge the work of The Partnership for 21st Century Skills. Please visit *www.21stcenturyskills.org* for more information.

CONTENTS

HOW DID THEY BUILD THAT?

STADIUMS ARE BIG BUILDINGS

A stadium is a huge building where people gather to watch an event. It might be sports or a music concert.

Some stadiums can hold the population of a small city! It might take years to build a new stadium.

This stadium is being used for a tennis match.

MAKE A GUESS!

Look around the next time you are in a stadium. Guess what sport is played there. Guess what other events happen there. Now ask your parents what events are held at the stadium. Did you guess correctly?

BUILDING BEGINS

First, workers dig holes for the **foundation**. The foundation keeps the building strong. It is made of concrete. Concrete is as hard as stone when it dries.

Cranes lift huge steel columns and beams. The columns and beams make the **frame** of the stadium. The frame is like the building's skeleton.

Cranes lift heavy objects. Workers could not lift the columns without cranes.

Masons work with stone and brick to build outside walls. **Electricians** put in wires for lights and computers. **Plumbers** put in pipes for water.

Electricians help put in stadium lights. Without lights, the stadium could not be used at night.

SEATING

Modern stadiums have seats. The seats are in long rows. Some seats are hard. Others have soft cushions. The largest stadiums have 100,000 seats or more!

Stadium seats have numbers on them. The numbers let people know which seat is theirs.

Workers place seats carefully. They need to make sure that everyone can see. Each row of seats is higher than the one in front of it. This is called **stadium seating**. This lets people in the back see over the people in the front.

Stadiums can be very crowded. If the rows were all on the same level, the people in back would not be able to see the action.

THINK!

Many movie theaters use stadium seating. The rows in front may all be on the same level. Why do you think some rows stay on the same level? Hint: do you know anyone who has trouble climbing stairs?

THE STADIUM ROOF

Most of us like to play our favorite sports outside. That is why many stadiums don't have roofs. Many sports are usually played outdoors. What do players do when the weather is bad?

Soccer is usually played outdoors, but it can be played indoors, too. This stadium with a roof has a soccer field inside.

Many new stadiums have **retractable** roofs. A retractable roof can open and close. It is left open when the weather is nice. It can be closed when it rains or snows. Some open in the middle like elevator doors. Others slide off in one big piece.

Millennium Stadium in Cardiff, Wales, has a retractable roof. It takes 20 minutes to open or close the roof.

LOOK!

Watch a sporting event on TV. Look carefully at the stadium. Does it have a roof? Can you tell if the roof is made to move?

THE PLAYING FIELD

Stadium builders have to decide what kind of turf to use. Turf covers the ground where sports are played. Some stadiums have turf made of natural grass. Other stadiums have **artificial** turf. Artificial turf is like a plastic carpet. It is strong and doesn't get muddy.

Artificial turf is often green and looks a lot like grass.

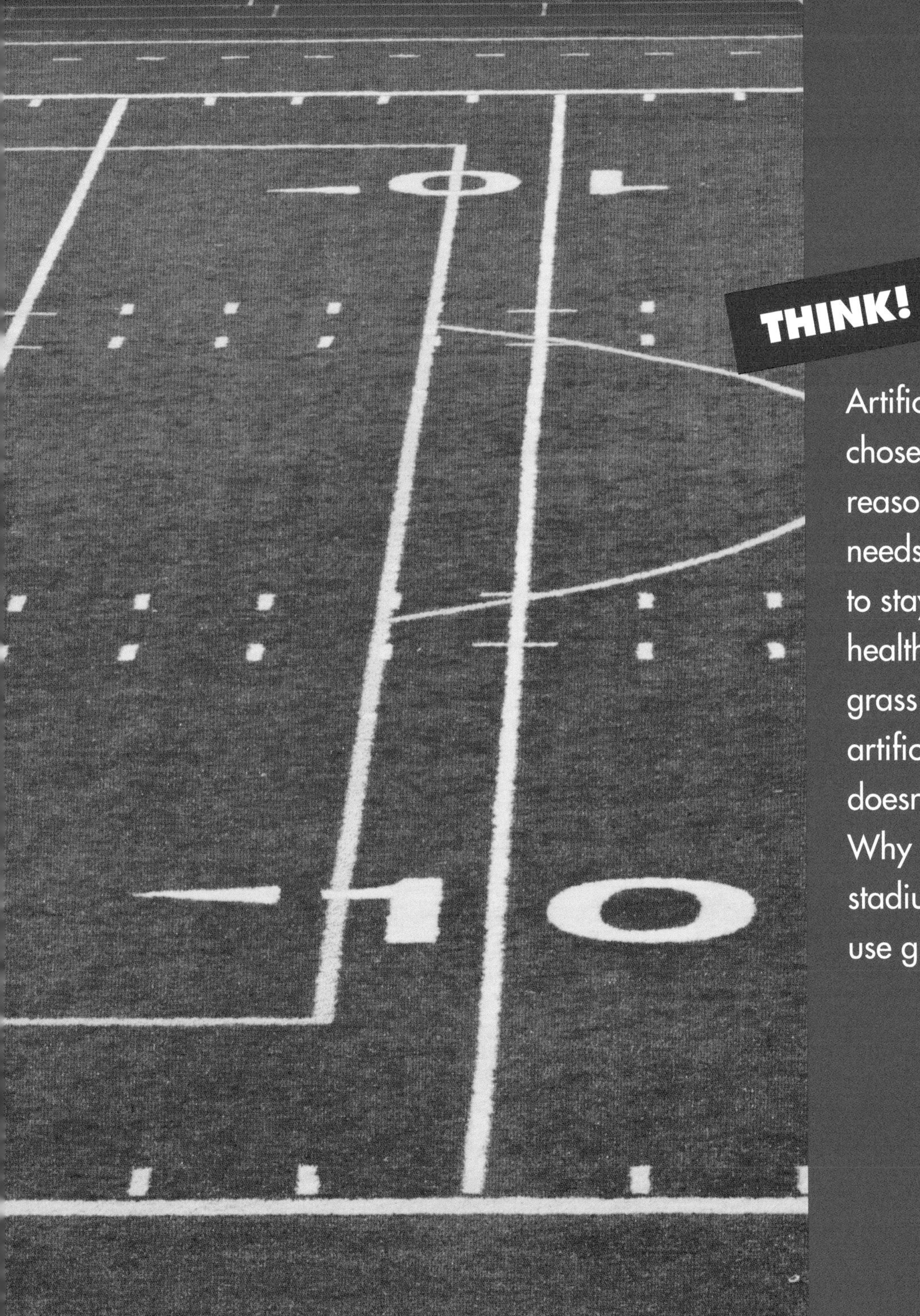

THINK!

Artificial turf is chosen for many reasons. Grass needs a lot of care to stay green and healthy. What does grass need that artificial turf doesn't need? Why do some stadiums still use grass?

The turf is down. Now the stadium is ready to open. People come from all over to enjoy events in the new building.

Look around the next time you go to a stadium. Now you know more about how the stadium was built!

People go to stadiums to enjoy sports or concerts.

FOX BOX
FASTSIGNS
Reliant Energy

GLOSSARY

artificial (ar-tuh-FISH-uhl) not natural; made by humans

cranes (KRAYNZ) machines used to lift heavy things

electricians (i-lek-TRISH-uhnz) people who install, maintain, or repair electrical wiring and equipment

foundation (foun-DAY-shuhn) a base on which something stands or is built

frame (FRAYM) the part of a building or structure that gives it shape

masons (MAY-sunz) workers who build with stone or brick

plumbers (PLUM-uhrz) people who install and repair sewer and water pipes

retractable (ree-TRAK-tuh-buhl) able to be pulled back

stadium seating (STAY-dee-uhm SEET-ing) seats placed in rows that rise higher the farther they get from a field or stage or screen

FIND OUT MORE

BOOKS

Curlee, Lynn. *Ballpark: The Story of America's Baseball Fields.* New York: Atheneum Books for Young Readers, 2005.

Oxlade, Chris. *Stadiums.* Chicago: Heinemann Library Publishing, 2006.

WEB SITES

KidzWorld.com—Dodger Stadium
www.kidzworld.com/article/15035-sports-venues-dodger-stadium
Fun facts about Dodger Stadium and links to information about other favorite sports stadiums

Washington State Public Stadium Authority—Construction Photo Gallery
www.stadium.org/photoGallery.asp?gallery=Construction
Photos of the construction of Qwest Field, home of the NFL's Seattle Seahawks

INDEX

ABOUT THE AUTHOR

Matt Mullins lives with his wife and son in Madison, Wisconsin. Formerly a journalist, Matt writes about science and engineering, current affairs, food and wine, and anything else that draws his interest.